D1827276

PRACTICAL LESSONS FOR EVANGELISM AMONG MUSLIMS

Vivienne Stacey

INTERSERVE
186 Kennington Park Road, London, SE11 4BT, UK

Published by
INTERSERVE, 186 Kennington Park Road, London, SE11 4BT

First Edition (English and German) 1980
First Indian Edition 1983   Both published in English by the
Second Indian Edition 1985   Henry Martyn Institute, Hyderabad
Revised English Edition 1988

ISBN 0 900165 18 9.

Printed in England by Wright's (Sandbach) Ltd., Cheshire.

CONTENTS

Vivienne Stacey, a partner with INTERSERVE,
has lived and worked in Asia and the Middle East since 1954.
She has taught, lectured and written
on the basis of her experiences and research.

Her books include biographies of Henry Martyn and Thomas
Valpy French.

This booklet is the first of the writer's 'Grassroots' series.

I. Communicating effectively with our Muslim friends.

We all probably meet Muslims from time to time. There are over 24 million in Europe and their number is increasing. Studies of contemporary international labour migrations in the Arab Middle East suggest that more trained personnel from Europe will work in the Middle East. So some of us will meet Muslims there. Others of us may join the missionary societies of the churches and serve in more traditional ways. So we need to consider how we may evangelise Muslim people whom we are constantly or regularly meeting. I am not speaking about the casual encounter but about continuing interchange and teaching. I suggest that to be effective communicators on this level, we must seek to work along the following lines.

1. SPEAKING THEIR LANGUAGE.

Obviously, it is not possible for everyone to learn Turkish or Arabic or Urdu, or some other language widely spoken by Muslims. If one learns even a little of one of these languages, it is very rewarding and helpful — and greatly appreciated by our Muslim friends. But however little or much we learn of their language, we may still fail to communicate on vital matters. It would be good if each Christian worked out his use of —

a: Greetings

In Pakistan, most Christians in the Punjab use the greeting *salam* rather than the more general greeting *as salam alekum*, to which the reply is *valekum as salam*. They therefore mark themselves as belonging to a sub-culture, and may be considered ill-mannered by the majority. *In this case everything is to be gained by conformity. No compromise is involved.* Christians sometimes refuse to use a perfectly good expression simply because Muslims use it. One example is the expression *in-shah-allah*, meaning 'God willing'. Sometimes when a Christian in the Punjab uses this expression, other Christians object. James 4:15 shows this idea to be Biblical, and so Christians could use it without compromise. It is well to reflect on such well-used words, their meanings and use.

b: Titles of respect for Muhammad and the Qur'an

My personal view is that, as Christians, we should give some title of respect to Muhammad. We may not want to call him a prophet, but we can use a word like *sharif*, which means 'noble', to describe him. Easterners are generally far more courteous and respectful than Westerners. So the question is how we can show respect without compromise. Likewise for the Qur'an, I would – in talking to a Muslim – use an adjective of respect like *majid*, meaning 'glorious'. In Urdu, *sharif* is often used of the Qur'an as well as *majid*. Likewise, we can give titles to Jesus and the Bible, for example, *Isa Al Masih* and the *Holy Bible*.

c: Appropriate terminology

I spent a month in Western India with some Hindi-speaking Christian Indians who were seeking to share the Christian message with their Urdu-speaking Muslim neighbours. With a little effort, they could alter some of their religious terminology to make it more relevant and acceptable to these Muslims. In essence, they had to drop a few words of Sanskrit origin and take Arabic words instead which were familiar to the Muslims.

For do this, they needed to be convinced of the need for this adaptation as a help in communication. For example, for the word 'love', they needed to drop *prem* and use *muhabbat;* for 'God', to drop *prebu* and use *Allah;* for 'peace', to drop the more usual word *shanti* and use *itminan,* etc. It was also important for them to learn to read Urdu as well as their own Hindi and Hindustani. This can be achieved easily by someone who is literate.

d: Jesus is the centre of the Christian message, so it is vital that the Muslim should know about whom we are speaking.

The name used for Jesus in the Qur'an is *Isa* (used 25 times). The title *Al Masih* is used eight times, and Jesus is sometimes called *Ibn-e-Mariam*, that is, 'son of Mary'. If the Christian identifies the Lord Jesus Christ with *Isa Al Masih* or *Ibn-e-Mariam*, the Muslim acquainted with the Qur'an will be in no doubt about whom we are talking. As good teachers, we can build on the known and go on to the (as yet) unknown.

e: Religious terminology

Here is a wide area for study, as Islam and Christianity have many terms in common but their definition can be quite different. It is easy to use the word *prayer* and to assume that it means personal talking to God and listening to him. For the Muslim, this would be *dua*, not the all-important *salat* or 'ceremonial' prayer. Words like *sin, repentance* and *salvation* are used in both the Bible and Qur'an, but their meanings are very different. It is vital to explore and explain the differences.

2. UNDERSTANDING THEIR CUSTOMS.

This is a vast subject. By observation, study and enquiry, we can come to a deeper appreciation and understanding of other people's customs.

Let me give one example. It is disrespectful for a Muslim to put the Qur'an on the ground or to treat it just like any other book. The Muslim often wraps up his Qur'an or puts it on a special stand. Christians should avoid offence in this matter in handling their own copies of the Qur'an, and should also treat their Bibles with respect. The contents of my suitcase are often examined by Muslim customs officials, so I am careful not to put my shoes near my Qur'an or Bible. Ideally, I have my shoes in another case. I pack both my Bible and Qur'an with special care.

3. THINKING THEIR WAY.

This generally means *thinking in an Eastern way*. If we continue thinking in our logical Western way, we may not be properly understood. We may fail to communicate the message we love best. One of my Pakistani friends, formerly Principal of a University college, said, "You Westerners, you leave nothing to the imagination!" We naturally think and discuss in logical terms. We think in steps and straight lines, not in circles. Truth, however, can be communicated and apprehended not only by logic and concept but by imagery, poetry and suggestion. It might be important to leave logical arguments and to present truth through parables, plays, proverbs, stories, poems and illustrations in the way that Christ often did.

a: Parables

It is not difficult to retell the Biblical parables in modern and Islamic dress. We need to prepare beforehand and to relate them to a Muslim rather than to a Jewish audience. The two men who went to the Temple to pray can become the two men who went to the mosque to pray at the call to prayer. The first man performed all the ablutions and ceremonial requirements but had his mind not on God but on the beautiful girl in the next house. The second man was so overcome by shame for his sins that he left out the ablutions and ceremonial requirements, and cried out to God for mercy. A Muslim hearing this story, asked to say whom he thought God would more readily accept, will often say that the first man gained God's favour, for he fulfilled the ritual.

This is the time to read or refer to the Biblical account and God's acceptance of the second man. Sin and the basis for forgiveness then become a fruitful and relevant discussion point, and by then we can certainly read the passage in its original form in Luke 18:9-14. If we had read or told it first in that form, it would not have been very meaningful or relevant to the Muslim.

We can also use these parables with children. Hearing the parables from their children at home, Muslim parents are unlikely to object or withdraw their children from Christian classes. An Asian acquaintance of mine who works among Muslims in a predominantly Muslim country drew up this series of parables that could be used with a Muslim enquirer up to his conversion — and beyond.

On sin —
   a) The Pharisee and the Publican: Luke 18:9-14.
   b) The Rich Fool (covetousness):   Luke 12:16-21.
   c) Ceremonial and real defilement: Matthew 15:1-20.

On God's love and our need to repent -
   a) The Lost Sheep: Luke 15:3-7.
   b) The Lost Coin: Luke 15:8-10.
   c) The Lost Son: Luke 15:11-32.

On the judgement of God -
   a) The Draw-net: Matthew 13:47-50.
   b) The Wheat and the Tares: Matthew 13:24-30.

On God's way for man's salvation -
   a) The Great Supper (the garment of righteousness):   Matthew 22:1-14.
   b) The wicked Tenants (God's provision of His Son):   Luke 20:9-18.

On counting the cost of following Christ -
   a) The Hidden Treasure: Matthew 13:44.
   b) The Precious Pearl: Matthew 13:45-46.
   c) The House Built on the Rock and the House Built on the Sand: Luke 6:48-49.

On Christian living and stewardship -
   a) The Two Debtors (forgiving others):   Luke 7:41-43
   b) The Unmerciful Servant (forgiveness):   Matthew 18:23-35.
   c) The Wise Steward (serving God):   Luke 12:42-48.
   d) The Pounds (serving God):   Luke 19:11-27.
   e) The Good Samaritan (love):   Luke 10:30-37.
   f) The New Cloth and the New Wine (new perspectives in life):   Luke 5:36-39.

   b: Plays

Dr Kenneth Bailey, in his book *The Cross and the Prodigal*, includes a play on the Parable of the Prodigal Son. A Christian youth group in Karachi, Pakistan, produced this play. During their practices, several Muslim friends asked if they might join the cast. The discussion about acting and presentation, and the very experience of taking on a part, proved to be a very convincing way for these Muslims to understand and enter into the truths of this parable. Early in this century, Temple Gairdner used plays in this way in Cairo. Maybe his casts were Christian, but the audiences were mostly Muslim. *Joseph and His Brothers* was particularly convincing in presenting the Christian message. Unfortunately, some other Christians in England queried his use of drama in evangelism, and his presentations were limited and restricted.

c: Proverbs

So often, quoting an apt proverb makes a spiritual truth come alive. It illustrates in a minute what may not be clear after ten minutes of logical presentation. The Urdu and Punjabi proverb that I use most is, "One fish makes the whole pond dirty". Such a proverb is helpful in explaining some of the effects of sin. See the story of Achan in Joshua 7. Most Eastern languages are rich in proverbs. We can learn some of them from the people themselves by asking about them and listening for them. The Biblical book of Proverbs deserves more study too. Let me give a few more Punjabi examples. There are many proverbs about hypocrisy, for example,"The Qur'an under his arm and his eye on the bullock" (that is, to steal it). Another suggestive proverb is, "Having eaten 700 mice, the cat goes to Mecca". Another is, "No theft, friendship or service takes place without a go-between".

d: Stories

It is wise to make a collection of stories to use in evangelism.

e: Poems

The Urdu radio programmes on FEBA Radio (Seychelles), based on the life of Jesus the Messiah, include many Urdu poems as well as songs. We could make use of poetry far more than we do.

f:Songs

It is often possible to communicate in song what would be unacceptable in conversation. Some friends of mine were camping in a remote valley in the north of Pakistan and had hired horses. The horse owner, who was a local leader, invited them to his home for a meal. My friends learned that the leader's father-in-law had been recently murdered. The visiting Christian woman tried to talk to the women about Christ's victory over death, but they were not keen to hear this message.

Then God guided her to sing. She has a lovely voice and she gave the same message in song. They asked her to sing again. Then she asked if she might pray for them. They asked her questions about the song. Two days later, two men came to ask the husband to sing for them. The words were very important to them. Because of this singing, the couple were invited to another meeting in the leader's house at which about thirty people had collected. Later, the leader and his son sought out my friend for a private chat and he told his brother in the city to get in touch with them there.

g: Illustrations

We must use illustrations which come out of the culture of our Muslim friends and out of their everyday life. One personal example may help. Some Pakistani village friends with whom I had been spending Christmas once put me on a local minibus. We were about eight miles from the city. The Volkswagen held about thirteen people, but three seats were empty.

Soon a farmer carrying a small bag got into the vehicle. The other passengers, who were also farmers, said, "What have you got in your bag?" He said, "Carrots." I said, "I don't have carrots in my bag." Of course, everyone wanted to know what was in my bag. After a suitable period of suspense, I said I had booklets in it, and then I passed them round. Several farmers read the tracts about the Lord Jesus, and one said, "This is foreign seed." I said, "Oh no! It is not foreign seed. It was first sown in Asia."

Then I was asked how long I had lived in Pakistan and whether I preferred living in Pakistan or England. I said, "When it is God's will for me to live in Pakistan, I like that best. When it is his will for me to live in England, I like that − but neither Pakistan nor England is really my country. I am just a traveller as we all are, and I am travelling towards another country." As Abraham demonstrated, we are 'strangers and pilgrims on the earth' (Hebrews 11:13-16). From this illustration, I could go on to explain more about the heavenly city and how one can get there safely. This way of thinking is not Western but it is meaningful to Easterners.

4.   USING THEIR POINTS OF CONTACT.

a: Amulets

Amulets or charms generally contain a paper on which is written a verse from the Qur'an. Christians sometimes declare that the wearing of an amulet is wrong and urge the person to take it off. Surely it would be better to enquire whether the person thinks God prefers his words to be round our necks or in our hearts. We can then share words of God which we have memorised and hidden in our hearts (Psalm 119:11).

b: The wearing of the veil (burqa)

Women often ask why we do not wear the veil. One answer is to spiritualise the matter and to say, "I wear a spiritual veil all the time." Of course, we have to give a full explanation. Isaiah 61:10 and Romans 13:14 will help us in this.

c: The creed

The Muslim who says so often, "There is no God but Allah, and Muhammad is his apostle" will sometimes ask us about his creed and ours. John 17:3 is a useful summary of the Christian creed as it speaks of the One God, of Jesus his apostle (or 'sent one'), and of knowing God.

d: Prayer

A discussion on prayer can lead us into an explanation of the Lord's Prayer which so many Christians pray every day (Luke 11:2-4).

e: Fasting

Especially during the fast of Ramadan, Muslims enquire from Christians about their beliefs and practices in regard to fasting. Isaiah 58 is a helpful passage to study and explain.

f: Almsgiving

The basis for Christian almsgiving and good works can be discussed (2 Corinthians 9:15).

g: Pilgrimage

John 14:1-6 describe the pilgrim, the pilgrim city and the pilgrim way. Jesus is the way (practice), the truth (belief), and the life (experience).

h: Other words

It is not always religious words which are points of contact. During the summer of 1978, a Pakistani fellow-traveller on the back of a Land Rover spoke of what Mr Zulfikar Ali Bhutto, the former Prime Minister, had done to help the remote northern regions of Pakistan in which we were travelling. He said that several people had volunteered to die in Bhutto's place. I asked him if he had ever heard of a completely innocent man who long ago was allowed to die in the place of others. This led on to some account of the death of Christ for us.

In conclusion, let it be said that to be effective communicators, we have to understand our Muslim friends' way of thinking. We have to enter into his mind, his heart, his emotions. "To the Jew I became as a Jew, in order to win the Jew; to those under the law, I became as one under the law − though not being myself under the law − that I might win those under the law. To those outside the law, I became as one outside the law ... that I might win those outside the law. To the weak, I became weak, that I might win the weak. I have become all things to all men, that I might by all means save some" (I Corinthians 9:20-22).

II. Evangelising and discipling our Muslim neighbours.

Let us be clear about our aims in evangelism. My primary aim in personal evangelism is to introduce my Muslim friend to my friend Jesus the Messiah, so that he or she can become a friend and disciple of Jesus and join the fellowship of his local disciples. This is likely to take place over a period of many times of sharing together. I am writing about a long and continuing relationship and not about a casual encounter on the street or in the train. I would have three subsidiary and contributory aims:

1 − To get my friend to read the Bible (or listen to it if he is illiterate).
2 − To pray with and for him in his presence when appropriate.
3 − To discuss and study the Bible and its message for us today together with him.

Prayer is in no way to be seen as a tool of evangelism. However, often in a crisis our Muslim friend will welcome our prayers and ask us or give permission for us to pray for him in the name of Jesus in his presence. I have Muslim friends in Bahrain who call the whole extended family together for me to pray with them all each time I visit them. It is their request. The way we pray naturally in private or in church may not be very appropriate in such a setting. I suggest that we should give more though to what we actually pray for and the terminology we use. If our preparation is thorough, the praying will be natural. Such a prayer could include:

— Praise of God: Muslims often praise God.

— Mention of the name of the person for whom one is praying: this will help the person named to realise God's nearness and personal concern.

— A small quotation from the Bible, especially from the words of a prophet like Isaiah or Jesus: Muslims esteem the actual words of a prophet very highly. The quotation should be appropriate to the prayer and not be used simply for evangelistic reasons.

— Mention of God's love: this is a very rare concept in Islam.

— Use of the name of Jesus the Messiah as a basis for offering the prayer: ask permission beforehand from your Muslim friend to offer the prayer in Jesus' name.

When lecturing last summer, I asked each of my Indian Christian students to prepare a prayer for use in the home of a sick Muslim friend. The best prayer was as follows:

"O God, Creator of the universe — You who created and now sustain all your creation with the word of your power: we worship you. We remember how great you are and yet how loving you are. There is no-one like you. We remember too that you are closer to us than our jugular vein. You know all things and so we are assured that you know each of us — our sin and our sicknesses. We thank you that you are able to deal with our sinfulness and heal our diseases. We remember the words that you spoke through your prophet Isaiah that all we like sheep have gone astray but you have laid our sins upon him, even Jesus, and by his being punished we are healed. Look in mercy upon this my friend who is ill and, according to your will and for your glory, heal him of his sickness and cleanse him from his sinful ways. We pray this in the name of Jesus the Messiah. Amen."

We need also to consider the *postures* we will adopt when we pray with Muslims. Will we use the standing position like

Solomon when he dedicated the Temple (1 Kings 8:22), or will we bow our heads before the Lord like Abraham's servant (Genesis 24:26)? Or will we follow the psalmist who calls us to kneel before the Lord as well as to bow down (Psalm 95:6)? Ezra fell on his knees and spread out his hands to the Lord (Ezra 9:5). In the Garden of Gethsemane, our Lord knelt in prayer (Luke 22:41). The Muslim who pays so much attention to the positions of prayer will watch us carefully and we should not put him off by our casual attitudes, and our lack of reverence expressed through bodily movements − or the lack of them. Not covering our heads when we pray may be very off-putting to Muslims.

When we get to the place of studying the Bible with our Muslim friend, the question arises as to what syllabus or set of studies we should use. *It is wise to stick to the text of the Bible, and not to use commentaries at this stage.* One of my former colleagues in the International Fellowship of Evangelical Students, Colin Chapman, prepared a set of ten subjects for study. The selection has been designed, first, as material to be studied with a Muslim in a regular systematic way; and, secondly, for a Muslim to read on his own.

The choice of subjects has been suggested by points of contact (eg 'God is one'), as well as by special problems (eg the avoidance of passages which speak of Jesus as 'the Son of God'). The subjects are arranged in a special order, starting with those which are less controversial but which deal with basic assumptions. Longer Biblical passages as well as a few individual verses are included, on the assumption that we should not rely on a few 'proof texts', but study verses in context as far as possible. The following are the ten subjects:

1. God is one.
2. God has made man in his image.
3. God has given man his laws.
4. God judges man for disobeying his laws.
5. God told his prophets that he would come among men.
6. The birth and ministry of Jesus.
7. The disciples came to believe that Jesus was the Messiah.
8. The Jews wanted to kill Jesus because of his claims about himself.

9. God raised Jesus from death.

10. God gives his Spirit to those who believe in Jesus.

Each subject forms one leaflet. All the Scriptural passages are introduced by a sentence or two to focus on the main relevance of the passage. Passages from the gospels are taken where possible from the Gospel of Luke.

Each leaflet ends with a prayer from the Bible. I give the first one here as an example (without the text):

1. God is One

The *tawrat* which was revealed to Moses forbids every kind of idolatry:

— the first two of the Ten Commandments declare that there is no god but God; and he alone is to be worshipped (Exodus 20:1-6).

— there is only One God, and we are commanded to love him (Deuteronomy 6:4-5).

The *prophets* repeatedly condemned idolatry:

— eg the prophet Isaiah argues that if we believe in one Creator God we cannot possibly accept the idea of idols (Isaiah 40:18-26).

When Jesus was asked which of the commandments in the Old Testament was the most important, he replied as in Mark 12:28-30.

The apostle Paul condemns idolatry with other serious sins (Galatians 5:19-21).

The apostle John includes idolatry among other deadly sins which deserve the judgement of God in Hell (Revelation 21:8).

The apostle John appeals to all believers to avoid any kind of idolatry (1 John 5:21).

Prayer: Psalm 95:1-7.

Having considered our main and subsidiary aims, and what we will do if we arrive at the latter, ie praying and studying the Bible with our Muslim friend, let us reflect on our ways of approach to our Muslim friends.

As Westerners, we have tended to prepare ourselves to meet the *theologically-minded* Muslim. We have often assumed that his greatest need is to be logically and intellectually convinced of the truth of the Biblical position. While this is so for some, very many Muslims have needs in relation not to intellectual queries but in the areas of superstition, fear, doubt, illness and death. They are looking for a Power that is greater than these fears, and which can deliver them. They want the security of a guide, protection against evil spirits and the evil eye, deliverance from fear of the future and death, healing from their diseases, etc. We enter then the world of *popular* or *folk* Islam, rather than Qur'anic Islam.

Recently I visited a Muslim shrine in India. A great Muslim religious leader or *pir* lay buried there. Muslims and Hindus come in numbers to the shrine to get healing from the spring water nearby which is said to have magical qualities. Others come to see the wonders done in the name of the 'saint'. I saw one 'miracle' performed — the raising of a rock weighing 50 kg to a height of four feet on the tips of five fingers (one finger per man). It was quite convincing but may have a scientific explanation. However, the purpose of the 'miracle' remains — to impress the humble worshipper with the power of the saint.

The best way that I can briefly give an introduction to the vast subject of popular Islam is to quote from Bill Musk's paper published in *The Gospel and Islam: A 1978 Compendium*, edited by Don McCurry, 1979. His paper is entitled *Popular Islam: The Hunger of the Heart*. In Diagram A on page 218 he contrasts between Qur'anic and popular Islam the meanings of the six articles of Muslim belief as follows:

Qur'anic Islam		Popular Islam
Monotheistic confession of faith	One God	Magical use of the names of God
Servants of God to do his will	His Angels	Demonology and jinn-worship
Encoding of God's self revelation	His Books	Bibliomancy (magical use of the Bible) and bibliolatry (worship of the Bible)
Vehicle of God's self revelation	His Apostles	Fetishes; worship of saints
Ethical focus of man's life	His Judgements	Spirit-life after death
Omnipotence of God	His Decrees	Used as sanctions by saints, sorcerers and other religious practitioners

Here are some examples of how popular Islam is practised:

One educated Muslim told me that his mother had put an amulet containing Qur'anic verses around the neck of his small brother, and that his brother had been wonderfully delivered from death on three occasions. He attributes this to the power of the amulet.

Many patients coming to the hospital where I live in the North West Frontier Province of Pakistan have already been to seek cures for their disease at shrines. They travel far to take offerings to and secure help from religious practitioners. Some are told to take a paper on which is written a verse of the Qur'an, put it in water and then, after some time, to give it to the patient to drink. For such a paper a charge is made by the religious practitioner.

A Muslim convert from Islam to Christianity told me how each year crowds come to the shrine where one of his ancestors is buried. They bring their offerings for the dead and the living, and expect to find blessing because of this. After the days of celebration, the family gathers to share out the offerings. Generally, there is a dispute about the distribution of the offerings. All this is part of popular Islam indicating needs which are more psychological than theological.

Many Muslim women are far more concerned about their sick children or possible divorce by their husbands than about the problem of understanding the Trinity or the Sonship of Christ. If, in a Christian's life under pressure, they see the power and grace of God and are attracted by Christian love and concern, they will be happy to hear about Christ the Healer and Saviour who loves all.

In India and Pakistan, there is a revival of 'Muhammad-veneration'. This again illustrates the hunger of the heart to come in contact with an exalted being who is not remote. For years I have puzzled over how to share the Gospel with a Muslim friend who so easily applied most of what I said about Christ to Muhammad. It seemed that I was helping her to be a more devoted follower of Muhammad rather than winning her towards Christ! When I stayed in her home for a few days, she lent me – among other books – a copy of her translations of the *Qasida Borda*. This *Qasida* was written in praise of Muhammad by Hazrat Imam Sharfuddin Busairi. The poet was born at Abusair in AD 1213. Here are a few verses about Muhammad taken from the poem:

Verse 34 — The holy prophet is the pious leader of both the worlds, king of mankind and Jinns, and monarch of all things that inhabit the universe.

Verse 35 — He is a prophet who clearly forbids us to do this, and commands us to do that. He has no parallel in all his teaching; he frankly either accepts or rejects statements.

Verse 36 — He is a well-wisher and a sincere friend, by whose intercessions we hope to have our salvation, on the day of judgement, when we have to face extreme agonies.

Verse 42 — No-one in the world can rival the qualities he possesses. He is the unparalleled jewel of beauty, which cannot be cut.

Verse 59 — He is indeed extremely lucky, who has smelt and kissed the hallowed dust of the grave of the monarch of mankind.

Verse 60 — At his birth all goodness and beauty saw the light of day. Pure was his beginning and pure was his end.

Verse 66 — The Jinns wailed, and luminaries were seen everywhere. The 'Noor' of Allah emanated from every word and sense.

We have to bear in mind Eastern exaggeration and poetic licence. Even so, the view of Muhammad presented in the poem belongs more to the resurgence of Muhammad-veneration found today than to the Qur'anic picture of him. My friend belongs to a sub-sect of the Shia branch of Islam. The Shias naturally tend to focus on a person or charismatic leader rather than on theology and doctrine. With Shias more so than with Sunnis (orthodox Muslims), there is every reason to present Christ as the suffering servant of God (Sura 19:31 and Philippians 2:7), who sacrificed himself for man's sin. *Suffering is a theme which recurs in Shia Islam.* My friend, commenting on some of our mutual Christian friends, said that what impressed her most about them was their spirit of self-sacrifice. Here than was my cue — not so much to present Christ as Lord of the worlds and King of kings, but as the sinless prophet whom God raised from the dead and vindicated (Philippians 2:5-11). The apostle Paul urges us to have 'the mind of Christ'. His mind is revealed in his taking the way of the Cross. His response to persecution was seen in the love which suffers.

Dudley Woodberry, formerly of the Christian Study Centre, Rawalpindi, Pakistan, once said in a lecture on Philippians 2, "Our Muslim friends may not be able to accept the Cross of Christ intellectually, but perhaps if they see us taking up our crosses daily and following him (Luke 9:23-24), they will be able to understand the same self-giving love which led him to his Cross."

Whatever interpretation we give to the Qur'an's words about the crucifixion, every Muslim would agree that the Qur'an accepts man's intention to crucify Christ. The Qur'an also accepts that Christ was willing to die. *The Muslim has a tremendous sympathy for Christ.* He understands something of his person and, recognising him as God's prophet and servant, wants to protect him from the shame of defeat.

I am convinced that the bridging between what the Muslim understands of Christ and the reality of his person and work is not just a matter of intellectual understanding. In these days of resurgent Islam, Christians have a unique opportunity to respond, not with countermoves or rival programmes, *but with the love which suffers and endures.* Christ's temptation was to avoid 'the cup' of suffering. He deliberately chose the way of the Cross. As his followers, so must we. Out of our weakness God will show his strength.

This non-verbal communication may speak more convincingly than intellectual argument. My friend may not understand the glory and greatness of Christ until she understands why he suffered. Muhammad-veneration and folk Islam are but the cries of the heart for one who identifies himself with us, 'a man of sorrows', who has borne the sins of many. So, in the end – for the Muslim – Christ is a friend misunderstood. It is our privilege to seek to introduce our Muslim friends to the Friend who 'sticks closer than a brother' because he is Redeemer and Lord and God.

III. Meaningful dialogue with Muslim students.

When Christ was on earth, he spoke in the context of Palestine during the imperialist Roman occupation of the first century AD. We may not know how he would have spoken to students. But we must consider how he might speak to the student world in this last quarter of the twentieth century with special reference to the Muslim student. Only the minority of Muslim students study abroad, *but they are for various reasons extremely strategic*. The Muslim student in a foreign university or college is aware of his need of friendship and of concern for his welfare — whether this is shown by Christians, Communists, or any other group or person.

I know of one national believer in a country where there is no visible church. He is praying that ten of his fellow-countrymen who are studying abroad will find Christ and return as his disciples. *God can use friendly Christians to answer this prayer*. The Muslim student abroad is more open, less on the defensive, and keener to understand new ideas and situations than he would be in his home country.

There is no typical Muslim student. We must ask: to which country does he belong? To which social stratum? Is he a Sunni? A Shia? Is he a member of some Shia sub-sect or some other group? Is he a practising Muslim or only a nominal one? Many national, cultural, social and religious influences have affected his development. Let us however divide Muslim students, wherever they study, at home or abroad, into 'religious' students and 'secular' students. I have met Muslim students who do not believe in God but who would still claim to be Muslims in a cultural and national sense. In a way, these Muslim atheists or agnostics are 'religious' rather than 'secular', for they are concerned with religion while rejecting the religious ideas of their fathers' faith.

But let us look at the truly 'secular' Muslim. He is a person who says that belief is entirely a personal matter governing one's private life. But such a concept is not properly Islamic and reflects 'secularisation' in Islam.

One of the most interesting examples of the 'secularising' trend in Islam is to be found in Algeria. The Algerian Constitution of 1976 declares Islam to be the religion of the state. The cultural revolution has as one of its particular objectives the adoption of a lifestyle in harmony with Islamic morals and the principles of the socialist Revolution, as defined by the national charter. The presidential oath includes the promise 'to respect and glorify the Islamic religion'. The French, however, ruled Algeria for well over a century and the present government obviously recognises the influence of French culture and literature.

European secular thought may be a more powerful influence on students than Islamic philosophy and literature. Yet the new educational reforms put a greater stress on Arabic, Arabisation and Islam. The question is, from where does the modern Algerian student draw his inspiration? Does he look to the Al Azhar and the Qur'an − or to Paris and modern European philosophy? It is interesting that two modern Algerian women writers who were elected to the Algerian Assembly write in French, not Arabic. In approaching Algerian students, the Christian may need to be more familiar with Jean-Paul Sartre and Albert Camus than with Al-Ghazzali.

One approach to the 'secular' or 'religious' Muslim student is through his own indigenous literature. Let me take one example from Pakistan and another from Egypt. Most Pakistanis hold Dr Muhammad Iqbal, the poet-philosopher, in high regard although he died in 1938, well before the creation of Pakistan. In Islam and beyond, he is a world figure who did much to show the relevance of Islam to modern life. Iqbal studied in Munich and was greatly influenced by some German philosophers. His one English work is *Reconstruction of Religious Thought in Islam.* Otherwise, his thought and influence are embodied in his great poetical works in Urdu and Persian. To approach Pakistanis, and especially students, without some firsthand knowledge of Iqbal and his poetry is like living in

24

Germany with no knowledge of Goethe or evangelising in England with no familiarity with Shakespeare.

The 'secular' student can be reached through Iqbal because he is such a great Muslim poet and philosopher. The 'religious' student can be reached through him for the same reason as well as for his religious thought. The Westerner who appreciates Iqbal has started to think in Eastern terms.

One Arab writer noted that Iqbal's poetry has five creative elements:

His firm faith.
The Qur'an.
His love of 'morning devotions'.
His philosophy of 'self'.
The influence of the poetry of Maulana Rumi, the famous Persian poet.

Iqbal's philosophy of 'self' can lead one into discussion on the nature of man. His frequent references to prayer and 'morning devotions' appeal to many Easterners even if they themselves are not as faithful as Iqbal in their practice. In a collection of poems called *Bal-e-Jibrael* ('The Wings of Gabriel'), Iqbal writes, "Whether it be Attar, or Rumi, or Razi, or Ghazzali, they cannot achieve anything without the early morning devotions." "Even in the sword-sharp cold wind of London, I never gave up my respected custom of early morning devotions." There are many other such references which remind one that the Bible is full of similar references to prayer in the early morning (eg 1 Samuel 1:19, Mark 1:35). The subject of Iqbal and prayer can be a fruitful point of contact with the religious Muslim who reads Urdu or Persian or both.

With the 'secular' Muslim, Iqbal's poetry and Rumi's poetry would also be a profitable line to pursue. In *Bal-e-Jibrael*, Poem 3, Iqbal wrote, "Your cure lies in the fiery but sad poetry of Rumi. (Your) disease is that you suffer from the magic of the Western thought which has succeeded in dominating your thinking." Rumi, like several other Sufi poets, makes significant references to Christ. I remember once at

Baghdad Airport having a conversation with a Pakistani student who had been studying in Munich. He was carrying as the most evident piece of his hand luggage a large piece of wood wrapped in cloth. On the wood, Sadiqain — Pakistan's leading artist — had painted a verse of the Qur'an. He proudly showed me and an Iraqi actress this treasure which was something from his culture as well as from his religion. I had been reading a history of Christians in Iran and was able to show him a quotation from Rumi about Christ. He was probably a 'religious' Muslim and the actress was probably 'secular', but Rumi proved to be a contact point with both. I have laboured this point as *we seldom take time to try to immerse ourselves in other people's heritages.* For this we are the poorer, and so is our witness. We do well to remember St Paul, who could quote the Greek poets (Acts 17:28) and the Cretan prophets (Titus 1:12).

My second example of the use of indigenous literature in the approach to Muslim students is from Egypt's leading playwright of today. Tewfik Al-Hakim's Arabic plays are read throughout the Arab world, and some are available in translation. Heinemann has published a collection of four. The earliest one, *The Song of Death,* "has as its central theme the conflict between traditional vengeance and freedom through education from such deadening and destructive prejudice." The play describes the dilemma facing a student from Cairo returning to his home village. For those who do not read Arabic, Heinemann has published *Modern Arabic Short Stories* (selected and translated by Denys Johnson-Davies, 1976), a selection by contemporary authors from several Arab lands including Egypt, Lebanon, Syria and Iraq. "They represent an interesting phase in the overall continuing resurgence of Arabic literature ... and give some indication of the way Arab men and women view the modern world."

Still another bridge in communication with all types of Muslim students is the study and use of proverbs. Speaking of the choice of priorities and the Pearl of Great Price (Matthew 13:45), one can quote the Urdu and Punjabi proverb, "If it is expensive, you weep once; if it is cheap, you weep many times." Here is a whole field for us to explore.

Last, but not least in importance, we should consider our use of religious vocabulary in discussions with Muslim students. On a plane from Delhi to a Central Asian city I was reading an English book called *The Islamic Tradition* by John B. Christopher (Harper and Row, 1972), and making notes in Urdu. The student next to me was fascinated.

Realising that I was intriguing her, I greeted her. She expressed her surprise that I was writing in Persian. I explained that I was really writing Urdu, but that the word *salvation* was written the same way in Urdu and Persian. I refrained from explaining *salvation* and prayed that she would enquire further if she was genuinely wanting to understand.

After lunch she again asked what in the world I was doing. I explained that I had noted the words *sin, repentance* and *salvation* in Urdu and I was studying their use in Islam and Christianity as, although the same words were used, the meanings were not the same. I explained the different concepts for the same words and asked if she had read the Bible, for she had told me that she was studying English literature. Apparently she had a Bible in English but had found it difficult to understand, so I suggested she start with Genesis and Matthew. She eagerly accepted my offer of a brief outline of the message of the Bible. I wrote this for her and she gratefully put it into her handbag before we parted. Meaningful dialogue with students must take into account this usage of the same religious terms but with different connotations and meaning.

To win Muslim students for Christ we need three things:

1. *A burden of prayer like St Paul's:* "My heart's desire and prayer to God for them is that they may be saved ... " (Romans 10:1-3; see also 9:1-3).
2. *A knowledge of Islam and Islamic literature* as well as a knowledge of our own faith and theology.
3. *An ability to communicate in meaningful terms,* appreciating that words like 'sin', 'repentance' and 'salvation' have very different meanings for the Muslim, and that concepts of the nature of man, the unity of God and prophethood are also very different in parts.

Prayer is a matter of the heart; knowledge, of the mind. Communication relates to the communing of man with man, a matter of the soul or spirit. To share the Gospel is to share Christ and to share ourselves.

IV. Meaningful conversations with Muslim women.

Christ's conversations with individual women showed that he respected and understood them as people, and appreciated their different religious and social backgrounds. He was also deeply aware of their psychological needs. One could profitably study his conversations with the Samaritan woman in John 4:1-42, with the woman taken in adultery in John 8:1-11, with Mary and Martha in John 11, with his mother in John 19: 25-27, and with Mary Magdalene in the garden after his resurrection – John 20:1-18. There are other examples in other gospels.

We must realise that, just as we saw that there was no typical Muslim student, so *there is no typical Muslim woman.* For meaningful conversation we must have some understanding of the background of the individual with whom we are talking. Let us assume that we are not referring to a casual encounter but that, on a basis of friendship, a Christian and a Muslim woman are getting to know each other and to share at more and deeper levels.

The Christian must understand the religious, social and psychological situations of her Muslim friend.

Is the Muslim woman we know devoutly religious, practising her faith and its requirements? To which sect of Islam does she belong? Is she a Sunni, a Shia, an Ismaili, or a member of some other sub-sect? Is she a Sufi? If so, what group of Sufis is she associated with? What does she know about the Christian faith? Has she, like some uneducated Saudi Arabian women, only just discovered that not all people are Muslim? Has she had previous contact with Christians? Or has she studied the Bible in connection with her studies of, say, English or German literature?

Is she illiterate? Is she well educated? If so, in what system? Is she an Algerian woman who has been exposed to French European culture, or has she been taught in an Islamic religious school in her home town? Is she naturally intelligent? Has she learned to think for herself? Is she an Indian Muslim — or is she Turkish, Indonesian, Omani? What is her country and to what section of the community does she belong?

What is the position of women in her country? Has she benefited from the relative freedom for women in a country like Tunisia, which was one of the earliest Muslim lands in its reforms — or does she belong to a country like Saudi Arabia where the constitution is the Qur'an? Is she from the rural areas or has she always lived in a city? What of her family setup? Is she married? What is her age? All these are legitimate questions to be kept in the mind of the Christian communicator.

Is our Muslim friend more concerned about her psychological fears than her intellectual questions (if any)? Maybe she is worried whether or not her husband will divorce her or take a second wife, about the dangers of childbirth, about the evil eye and the antagonistic forces of the spirit world. In Algeria, maraboutism (the veneration of saints) is forbidden by law but many women still go to religious leaders and seek help through ancient practices and superstitions. There is a considerable influence traceable to animism rather than Islam.

Briefly, we have been able to see some of the complex factors which influence an individual. Even such a cursory study should make us aware that there are many kinds of Muslim women. Similarly, there is not just one approach or method to be followed in conversation and discussion about the Christian Gospel. *There are many methods and approaches.* Let us look at three — recitation, song, and key words.

Recitation and Song. The word *Qur'an* means 'recitation'. The Qur'an in Arabic is to be recited aloud or chanted and memorised. It is difficult for the Westerner with his emphasis on reading rather than listening to appreciate what the chanting of the Qur'an means to the devout Muslim. Words and sounds of classical Arabic recited by a gifted speaker may be more significant than an intellectual appreciation of the meaning. Let me give an example of how this approach has been adapted for use with some Central Asian nomads who had crossed into Pakistan at the end of the winter.

Two of their women in need of medical treatment were admitted, along with their families, into a Christian hospital. One day the doctor heard them singing a song about the Gulf oil state of Qatar. The dialogue in the song went like this:

Husband: "I am going to Qatar and I will bring you back lots of green, green notes."
Wife: "Don't go there. You will have many troubles in Qatar. If God can provide daily bread for you there, why can't he continue to provide it for us here? Don't go to Qatar."

Apparently, this Muslim family make up songs like this round their camp fire in the evenings. One woman asked the doctor to sing one of her songs. So she made up one in Pushtu about the Parable of the Feast, based on Luke 14. The excuses she gave for not coming to the feast were ones her patients often use when they do not want to be admitted as in-patients. The song was composed and sung originally by the Medical Mission Sisters in Pakistan. This is an adapted version by the doctor mentioned above:

Chorus:

I cannot come
to your feast to which I have been invited.
My buffaloes will not yield their milk to anyone else.
I have lots of little children at home and my house is isolated.
Therefore I beg to be excused — I cannot come.

There was a man who held a feast in his house.
He invited many people and sent a servant
To say to the people — The food is ready.
But at once they all began to make excuses.

I cannot come, etc.

When the master heard these things he became angry
And said to the servant — Go to the Bazaar
And bring here the poor, lame, paralysed and blind,
My house must be absolutely full.

I cannot come, etc.

In this parable the Lord Jesus gives us a lesson,
That when God calls, we should listen
And obey and accept whatever He says,
So that we may obtain eternal life and salvation.

I cannot come, etc.

The woman listened attentively and questioned and asked to
have the song written down so that they could sing it at home
round the camp fire. So the doctor wrote it down and gave
them the booklet in which the episode is recorded — the
Gospel of Luke. The second family asked for a song also. So
the doctor gave them another song based on Matthew, along
with a copy of the Gospel and a written song. Both families
were to use the songs, and a literate member was to read the
gospels aloud, so the good news would be spread through
indigenous methods of communication.

Prayer is a natural human expression. Muslims are deliberate in
their emphasis on regular prayer *(salat)* as well as on more
impromptu or personal prayer *(dua).* In crises or on special
occasions, a Muslim may request her Christian friend to pray
for her. Several of the Christian midwives I know find their
Muslim patients naturally nervous of the dangers of childbirth
but also fearful, because of the superstitions and practices
which are part of their culture. They sometimes request these
midwives to pray. Sometimes, after a delivery, the Christian
midwife can talk along the following lines:

*"You are now the mother of a new baby. God has brought him (or
her) safely into this world and has kept you safe too. Let us thank
God for His love and goodness to you, and for bringing this new life
into your family. Jesus Christ the eternal Lord and Saviour of the
world was born as a baby just like yours. His mother Mary
experienced the pain of labour as you have, and rejoiced in the birth*

of her new baby as you have. Jesus Christ came into this world to save us from sin and to make us righteous before God. God has given physical life to you and your baby by the process of natural birth. He also wants to give spiritual life by the process of spiritual birth which comes through faith in Jesus Christ."

A suggested prayer for use at the birth of a child is: *"O Creator God, we thank you that through your goodness this child has been safely born and that the mother has been freed from suffering. Now we beseech you that these to whom you have given physical life may also obtain spiritual life through the sacrifice of Jesus Christ. Amen."*

Key Words: Christ used key words to make a link between everyday familiarities and spiritual truth, as we see in the story of his conversation with the Samaritan woman where the key word was *water*. Once I had a conversation in a Punjabi village with a woman who enquired how many houses I owned. At first I said none, but then she claimed that her extended family or clan owned two hundred houses. Then I told her that my extended family owned more than that. She became really interested when I explained that the houses were so secure that there was no danger of robbery and no need of repair. "In my father's house are many mansions." I offered to read about these houses, and she listened carefully to John 14:1-6. The key word was *house*. Other key words from daily life can be used. There are also many religious terms which can be used as points of contact, eg *pilgrimage, fasting, creed*. Such terms lead to a more intellectual and theological discussion. Some Muslim women benefit from such discussion. On the whole, women talk with women and men with men in Muslim society — but sometimes couples can discuss with other couples. In all such conversations, we will need to draw on all the educational, cultural and other experiences with which God has prepared us. Supremely, after diligent preparation, we rely on the Holy Spirit. He alone leads us and any others into truth and to Jesus Christ the Lord.

A Finnish proverb states that 'The workman is trained by his work.' This saying is a reminder that lessons and guidelines may be helpful but, as a believer shares his faith with prayer, constrained by love and guided by the Holy Spirit, he learns what to do in every situation. From his experiences and in the light of Scripture, and with an awareness of the cultural and religious situations of his Muslim friends, he moves out with God into what is frontier territory. May we experiment creatively as we seek to communicate.